101
ways
to know you're
"black"
in
corporate america

To Ruth
Continue
to Keep your
eyes on the
"True"
prize
Be Blessed

MW00791432

101

ways
to know you're

"black"

in

corporate america

you know you're black in
corporate america when...

*A collection of moments capturing what it's really like,
with powerful words of inspiration for your success.*

Deborah A. Watts

Watts - Five Productions

Printed in the United States

Published by Watts-Five Productions
1400-F Hwy 101 North Suite 117
Plymouth, Minnesota 55447-3064
Book layout and typeset by Melvin Carter III and Parker Initiatives Publishing
Cover design by Associates by Design
Cover illustration by Ta-coumba T. Aiken

Library of Congress Catalog Card Number 98-90708
ISBN: 0-9666276-0-1

First Edition

Dedication

In memory of my great-grand parents Joseph and Mattie Smith who left a legacy of family first, passion, self-determination, and love, also Emmett Till my cousin whose untimely death inspires a search for hope.

To those who are in corporate America, striving, surviving, achieving and succeeding. To those who are challenged with self doubt and frustration. To those who have played the game and won and to those who have played and lost. To those who chose not to play at all. To those who can laugh at their experiences and to those who can't. Finally to those major and minor corporate game players for without your reflections there would not be a book like this.

Acknowledgments

Thank you to the Father, Son and Holy Spirit for moving in my life, sweeping me off of my feet and taking the lead in controlling my life experiences. Thank you for sending your angels my way to protect, guide and encourage me to press on. Thank you for giving me the opportunity to experience success in corporate America and for providing the stepping stones needed to build the bridge for the next phase of my life. Thank you for allowing me this opportunity to share these reflections with others so that they can begin to build bridges in their lives as well.

Thanks to the many contributors who took time out of their busy schedules, allowing me to capture their reflections and experiences of being "black" in corporate America.

To those who gained at the expense of others, for the debt you owe is yet uncollected.

Thanks to those in corporate America whose eyes can see the many gaps in the bridge of understanding, and who know that the job of a bridge builder will be needed for long time.

Acknowledgments

Many thanks to Toni Carter of Parker Initiatives Publishing who served as advisor, engineer and consultant, your timely direction and insight provided the framework to make this book a reality. LeClair Lambert, my editor whose gift of giving life to my words helped to give meaning to my thoughts. Tacoumba Aiken, a rare gem whose spirit-filled gift of art was a catalyst to launch the pursuit of my passion. Dr. Earl F. Miller, for inspiring my soul with the word of GOD, Iyanla Vanzant for igniting the "power" within me. The International Leadership Institute and the Minneapolis University Rotary Club, whose support has enhanced my growth and expanded my horizons.

A million thanks to Paul Bryant, Janis Davis, Sandra Freeman, Robbin Frazier, Anna Hyde, Dr. Phil Layne, CeLois Steele and Charles Walton for your continued counsel and support. A special thanks to the many family members and friends who have provided support and encouragement to make this dream a reality. I could not have completed this project without you.

Special gratitude to Randy - my partner in life, best friend and husband - for your support and love. My children, Teri, Tia and Toni and my grandson, Marlon, who are the beats of my heart. My mother Doris and father AJ (deceased) for always believing, trusting and loving me unconditionally.

Table of Contents

Foreword

In America the individual is the "building block" to greatness. Yet, skin color has always been the determining factor in how much "building" will be tolerated. Deborah has skillfully used satire to trick corporate America into taking another look at itself. Instead of accepting the contributions so generously offered by Black Americans—the unwarranted fear of being upstaged has caused corporate America to wrap its ambitious undertakings in the barbed wire of hatred, depleting the self-confidence of the giver and robbing itself of the benefits. Both are losers.

May this two-edged sword of truth pierce the armor of racism, rendering it intolerable, making it possible for true greatness to prevail! For "true greatness equals true freedom."

America let's not forget that 43 years ago, I lost my son, Emmett Till. I'll never know what he would have become. His opportunity to contribute ended

at age 14, because of hate. How do we know what others would have become? How many other contributors have wound up "at the end of a rope?" From the loss of my son in Money, Mississippi to James Byrd in Jasper, Texas to the loss of talent and dreams in corporate America, not much has changed. The years have passed and progress has been made, but we are still faced with the same issue - racism. From the most entry level positions to the boardroom, people of color in corporate America are the newly disenfranchised. How many brilliant stars are too soon dimmed by the clouds of neglect and bias which act to dull their shine.

Wake up America! Not just Black America. Enough is enough! It's time for a change in all arenas. It is time for us to begin to work toward achieving the true greatness that we so proudly claim. This book provides an avenue for corporate America to start the process, by taking action now!

I am reminded of a quote by Derek Grier, editor of the magazine *A Word to the Diaspora,* "As action without compassion is cruel, mere sympathy without action is worthless."

Mamie Till Mobley

Preface

101 ways to know you're black in corporate america was written to begin a process of healing and generate hope for people of color, whose voices have been silenced by the shame, guilt and embarrassment of their corporate experiences.

This book attempts to capture those realities in a painfully humorous way. The intent is to expose the incidents of corporate racism and the issues relating to the cultural mythology of "white privilege" on a much different level than the more traditional, academic manner presented in many of the related studies and published literature that now exist. According to the Glass Ceiling Commission report " *A Solid Investment: Making Full Use of the Nation's Human Capital*", invisible barriers for individuals of diverse racial and ethnic backgrounds do exist throughout most workplaces. The report also notes that these barriers result from institutional and psychological practices that prevent qualified individuals from advancing within their organizations and reaching their fullest potential. Robert B. Reich, U.S. Labor Secretary and chair of the Glass Ceiling Commission said "The Glass Ceiling is not only a

setback that affects two-thirds of the population, but a serious economic problem that takes a huge financial toll on American business." Organizations like the National Black MBA Association (NBMBAA) have made great strides in increasing and improving their employment programs to assist corporations in successfully recruiting members of their organizations. In the January 1998 issue of the Black MBA Magazine, Antoinette Malveaux, Executive Director NBMBAA said "The recruitment or selection process [for African Americans] has improved over the past few years and can be qualified as extremely positive. However, once hired, African Americans often find that the attitudes of their bosses and coworkers contrast sharply with those exhibited when the company was courting."

Some of you are asking, why? Why the barriers? Why the exclusion? The roots of exclusion may be deeply embedded in the minds of corporate executives, directors, managers, supervisors and coworkers whose office is located next door to yours. Antoine Rutayisire, team leader for African Evangelistic Enterprise in Rwanda, explained that the root of exclusion stems from the differences in us. These differences often produce a feeling of fear, fright,

uncertainty and suspicion. The result of those feelings is self-protection. Let's face it! Most forms of discrimination, segregation, even hate crimes are all based on fear. "Some of the causes of the barriers of separation among people are as varied as our racial, social, economic origins, our cultural backgrounds, our intellectual levels of education, our life habits, political opinions, our life aims and aspirations, religious convictions and traditions and even our individual temperament. The smallest differences can cause alienation in human relationships." says Rutayisire. Believe it or not the feeling of fear occurs behind the walls of corporate America.

This book is written to challenge corporate leaders to acknowledge the realities that exist in their organizations. It exhorts them to openly discuss the issues and begin building the bridges of understanding by erasing the invisible lines that are drawn. And while they are accomplishing this, shatter the glass ceiling! "If America's businesses fully utilized the nation's human capital, they would be making a solid investment. For real change to occur, bias and discrimination must be banished from the boardrooms and executive suites of corporate America." states Reich. This book is designed to motivate everyone to move beyond inventing a better past. What is done is done. The past cannot be changed. But we can create a better vision for the future.

Introduction

*You know you're" black" in corporate America when you begin to rational-
ize racism, and when you ask the painful question, "when is enough, enough?"*

People of color often face chaotic, confusing and unclear illusions when behind the walls of corporate America. The faces, opportunities, ambitions,
aspirations, goals and allies can change right before your eyes. What looks
like it is usually isn't, and what seems like it will usually won't.

This book is a collection of 101 personal situations, moments and incidents
that have been experienced by some of the most brilliant and talented African
Americans working within the confines of corporate America. The 101 are
selected from a series of discussions, interviews and private conversations
conducted by the author. Each person was asked to complete the following
phrase....... "You know you're black in corporate america when......" Though
presented satirically, each of the 101 provides a picture of reality commonly
faced in corporate America by people of color.

Sit back and relax. You are about to open the door to corporate America. Close your eyes and listen to the sounds of the color game being played right in front of you. Some of you will laugh, relate to, empathize with, and perhaps be reminded of those most frustrating, embarrassing and painful times. Some of you will be awakened. Most of you will remember when........

This book is a collection of special moments in time when talented, eager and unsuspecting men and women have experienced the corporate color factor. Those who are black, red, yellow or brown can relate to or have an idea how this game is played. Simply it is played on those who are different. At any given moment, and without notice, the game begins and you could be the target. At any moment in time any of you could be "black" in corporate America.

Read this book with an open mind. Note those incidents that you've experienced, highlight those circumstances where you were a player in the game. Ponder those situations that you witnessed happening to others. Many of you have kept these memories tucked away, never intending to discuss them.

Yet, your experiences have had a plus or minus impact on your productivity, relationships, self esteem, economic stability, and career. Hopefully *101 ways...* will break the silence that now exists and open the door to more meaningful discussions about race. America needs someone to take action. Use this book to engage and explore with someone who may be "black" in corporate America.

Deborah A. Watts

101

ways
to know you're

"black"

in
corporate america

You know you're "black" in corporate america when...

Your name is first on the routing slip but you are always last to get the mail.

You know you're "black" in corporate america when...

You have been given a cream assignment. Your peers even ask how you were selected for such a key position. Later, you find that you have no power, resources or support. The project is out-of-step with the corporation's goals.

You are expected to fail.

You know you're "black" in corporate america when...

A white coworker sees you and several black colleagues at a casual lunch. Back at the office later he asks, "What was that meeting all about?"

You know you're "black" in corporate america when...

Your supervisor reviews all of the letters you write, marks the corrections in red, and leaves them on your desk where all can see. Your peers' corrections are always discussed in private.

You know you're "black" in corporate america when...

After graduating from college with Summa Cum Laude honors, you are offered an entry level job at one of the local corporations. Surprise, surprise, your manager happens to be one of your low achieving classmates who was hired into the company's fast track program.

You know you're "black" in corporate america when...

You arrive five minutes early for a 9 a.m. meeting scheduled weeks ago, your colleagues are already seated and the meeting is in progress. Your manager stops in mid-sentence and says, "You are an hour late. Didn't you get the notice I sent changing the time of the meeting? Have a seat!"

You know you're "black" in corporate america when...

You are hired for your decisiveness and toughmindedness and are soon asked to handle the next wave of downsizings and benefit reductions. At the end of the year recognition dinner you are rewarded with a sizable bonus and the company's presidential award. The next day you view a new organization chart of your department to find that your name does not appear.

Mission accomplished......task done........service no longer needed!

You know you're "black" in corporate america when...

Your credentials and effectiveness are questioned by a new Vice President who has been in position for only six months and is unaware of your consistent, stellar performance and great reputation. Your last twelve months of accomplishments are dismissed.

You know you're "black" in corporate america when...

You arrive at work on time as usual. Your boss, making her rounds, peaks in and remarks with surprise. "Oh you're here!"

You know you're "black" in corporate america when...

A colleague says with a broad smile, "You know, I really like you. When I see you, I don't see color. I don't think of you as black."

You know you're "black" in corporate america when...

You and three other white peers are given two year rotational assignments in different states. After five years you learn that they have all been reassigned to new, challenging positions and promotions back at headquarters. When you inquire about your status, you are told that movement is frozen except for special cases.

You know you're "black" in corporate america when...

You are promoted to an officer position and should be entitled to all perks. However, you and your team aren't allowed to ride the corporate jet.

The policy has recently changed.

You know you're "black" in corporate america when...

You are in the breakroom reading the book <u>The Spook Who Sat by the Door</u>. A coworker comments, "Gee, I like ghost stories too!"

You know you're "black" in corporate america when...

After an uncomfortable staff meeting, your boss suggests, "You need to work at making others more comfortable with you ....why don't you smile more often?"

You know you're "black" in corporate america when...

You make an important presentation to the company's executive board, but all the questions are directed to your white male assistant.

You know you're "black" in corporate america when...

You express displeasure about the confederate flag hanging on the wall at your coworkers' favorite restaurant. They reply, "But, the food is really great here, you should try the special!"

You know you're "black" in corporate america when...

You arrive at the airport baggage claim area, dressed in a navy blue suit, all ready for an important client meeting. A woman, taps you on the shoulder and without looking directly at you, says "Can you help me with my luggage?"

You know you're "black" in corporate america when...

You and a white colleague announce within days that you are leaving the company. He is given a big going away party at a nice restaurant. You get a card and a few "Good Lucks."

You know you're "black" in corporate america when...

You've been transferred to a new department. Your manager tells you he's selected the perfect person to train you in. He suggests you'll have a lot in common and learn a great deal from this person. When you meet your "trainer", he is an African American, with a dissimilar job, background and experience level.

You know you're "black" in corporate america when...

You unexpectedly returned early from a meeting and you find two colleagues leaving your office. They offer the excuse, "We were just admiring your family photos." You notice immediately that your middle desk drawer has been left open.

You know you're "black" in corporate america when...

A client you've never met is escorted to your office. With a startled look she says...... "Oh! Your voice sounded so different over the phone."

You know you're "black" in corporate america when...

Your colleague notices a photo of your 10 nieces and nephews and asks, "Just how many children do you have?"

You know you're "black" in corporate america when...

You bring a food item for the office food day and at end of the day none of it is eaten.

You know you're "black" in corporate america when...

You attend an office party where drinks are served. When your colleagues become tipsy, the males want to dance with you and the females want to dance with your spouse.

You know you're "black" in corporate america when...

You are discussing a work project with another black coworker. A white coworker interrupts and says "All right you guys, that's enough socializing. Get back to work."

You know you're "black" in corporate america when...

After three consistently successful years with your company, you make it clear during your performance review that you would like to seek greater responsibility and a promotion. Your director informs you that in order to reach that next slot, sales experience is a must. You take a job that gets you that experience. After two years, you are told that marketing experience is a must. You take a job that gets you that experience. After 2 years, you are told finance experience is a must. You take a job that gets you that experience.

... and on and on and on ...

You know you're "black" in corporate america when...

Your secretary is asked frequently by others, "What is it really like to work for a black person?"

You know you're "black" in corporate america when...

You and a colleague are seated at a table near the kitchen at a restaurant you've visited before. Your lunch partner naively remarks, "Don't take this personally, but have you ever noticed that every time we eat here, we are seated in the same section?"

You know you're "black" in corporate america when...

You discover in an informal conversation that your annual salary is less than any of your peers.

You know you're "black" in corporate america when...

You are on a business trip. You arrive at the hotel before a white colleague does, but no room is available for you. Your colleague arrives and is registered in. When the desk manager is told that both registrations were made at the same time, he says, "Oh, there must have been a computer error." Miraculously, a room becomes available.

You know you're "black" in corporate america when...

You are the first to board the corporate jet with a group of fellow executives. You take the closest seat facing forward, the others take seats in the rear. Your President boards, stands directly in front of you, and clears his throat several times.

You get the hint.

You know you're "black" in corporate america when...

You are more than qualified for a specific job and are asked frequently by others how you got the job. "Who do you know to have lucked up on such an opportunity?"

You know you're "black" in corporate america when...

You tell your supervisor about a problem you are having with a coworker. The response you get is "You've got to be exaggerating! It's hard to believe that about her. She is such a good worker."

You know you're "black" in corporate america when...

You get a high profile project, and your colleagues stop inviting you to lunch.

You know you're "black" in corporate america when...

You've been ill at home with the flu for a week. Your supervisor, who has never visited before, appears at your house with a bouquet of flowers— "just to cheer you up."

You know you're "black" in corporate america when...

A manager from another department informs your supervisor about a problem in your work group. When you question why you were not approached, you are told that the manager was afraid of "how you would respond."

You know you're "black" in corporate america when...

You call a prep meeting with your staff in your hotel room. They all comment on how small your room is. One says, "Who did you upset to deserve this closet?"

You know you're "black" in corporate america when...

Your manager repeatedly tells you that no one is holding you back.

You know you're "black" in corporate america when...

You are told that you are "rough around the edges" despite your completion of many professional development programs. A-N-D it is suggested that you should emulate the behavior of a 22 year old white female.

I DON'T THINK SO!!

You know you're "black" in corporate america when...

You and other coworkers attend the annual Martin Luther King Day Banquet. The guest gospel choir moves the audience with its great voices and music. Others clap and sing along with the choir, but not your colleagues. The only sound coming from your table is the tapping of your foot.

You know you're "black" in corporate america when...

You continually get more responsibility, but no authority.

You know you're "black" in corporate america when...

It is automatically assumed that you do not play golf, racquetball or ski. So why expect an invitation?

You know you're "black" in corporate america when...

You've just accepted a new sales position and you are given the worst area of the city, where no one has made a sale. You are told that it will be a challenge, but that you will do well.

You know you're "black" in corporate america when...

You are being recognized at an all company banquet. As you approach the stage to receive your company's highest achievement award, your corporation's top executive exclaims, "Yo, homeboy. Congratulations!"

You know you're "black" in corporate america when...

You are the only black executive leaving for an important trip with your director and colleagues, but the corporate jet is grounded due to foggy conditions. The group rents a van. You are the first one asked to drive.

You are not surprised.

You know you're "black" in corporate america when...

As an officer of the company, you are expected to be a member of the most exclusive country clubs in the city. The acceptance for all others requires one sponsor. You are told that you need several sponsors, many letters of recommendations and unanimous approval.

You know you're "black" in corporate america when...

You go through a long, grueling training course, and your peers continually ask others about your progress. When you return, after successful completion, no one says a word to you about it.

You know you're "black" in corporate america when...

You leave the building late at night with two colleagues. Armed with files and a briefcase, you are the only one stopped by security to show identification.

You know you're "black" in corporate america when...

You are hired as a new manager but are given only a superficial orientation, with no training and no plans for development.

You know you're "black" in corporate america when...

A new colleague of Jamaican descent informs you that he finds it odd to be required to show his driver's license and auto insurance in order to maintain employment, while two new white colleagues were not.

Welcome to America!

You know you're "black" in corporate america when...

Everyone leaves for lunch. With no offers from anyone, you are left sitting at your desk.

You know you're " black " in corporate america when...

You've been on a much deserved vacation for a week and return to find out that your mail is being routed to your boss.

You know you're "black" in corporate america when...

You are asked by a colleague during a one-on-one diversity training planning session, if he can "speak freely about all of this diversity - perversity stuff..." You are informed that it is "a waste of time. No one really cares, and since the company pays lip service to it anyway, let's just go have a drink."

You know you're "black" in corporate america when...

You are asked by a seasoned manager, known for her no-nonsense manner, to share some insight on a nonperformance issue related to an employee of color. Admitting to being afraid to handle the situation alone, she says "I need your help. You have a better understanding of how to communicate with *them*."

You know you're "black" in corporate america when...

You arrive at an off-site business retreat dressed in business casual attire. Your white peers approach and ask why you are always "s-o-o-o dressed up?"

You know you're "black" in corporate america when...

You make a rare visit to a different department on another floor to discuss a project with a colleague. Before you get back to your office, you are stopped and interrogated by a security officer.

You know you're "black" in corporate america when...

You are continually asked by your coworkers if your background ever gets in your way.

You know you're "black" in corporate america when...

You and a group of colleagues are on a road trip to a business meeting when you stop in a small town for breakfast. You and another coworker pause in the vehicle to go over some notes. Once you are seated with the group, you are apologetically told that the kitchen is closed. The group eats.... you and your colleague eat later at a nearby fast food restaurant down the street.

You know you're "black" in corporate america when...

You find that your salary and benefits are lower than that of your white peers who were hired at the same time.

You know you're "black" in corporate america when...

You are told you are decreasing your effectiveness with your "aggressive style" even though "aggressive risk taking" is a corporate value.

You know you're "black" in corporate america when...

Your son receives a four year academic scholarship to Dartmouth, and your manager asks " What sport does he play?"

You know you're "black" in corporate america when...

You are new to the company and you successfully complete a project in record time. Your supervisor is shocked and wonders out loud if you had any "outside help." The same afternoon you receive a memo warning you that all projects you work on require confidentiality and are not to be shared with any one outside your immediate group.

You know you're " black " in corporate america when...

You are frequently asked why you change your hairstyle so often.

You know you're "black" in corporate america when...

You are out of town and you try to rent a car with the company credit card. Colleagues in line before you are asked only to show their drivers license. You are asked for three forms of ID, to prove that you are who the card says you are.

You know you're "black" in corporate america when...

Your manager tries to convince you that she is not racist. She even adds "Some of my best friends are black."

You know you're "black" in corporate america when...

You must always perform at a higher standard, while your peers enjoy the same job with a higher salary and more perks.

You know you're "black" in corporate america when...

You receive a negative peer performance review. You are told that maybe ".... you are not a team player and try to 'outshine' your peers too often." It is suggested that you delay completing a few of your high priority projects "...and let them catch up. It will help improve relationships."

You know you're "black" in corporate america when...

You are told by your manager not to select any "soul food" for your 10 year anniversary party. "You know that kind of food is just too rich for our stomachs."

You know you're "black" in corporate america when...

You catch hell from your colleagues for being in the 'spotlight' just a little too much.

You know you're "black" in corporate america when...

A section of your floor houses several black employees, and you overhear your immediate coworkers call it "Nigga Row."

You know you're "black" in corporate america when...

Your young, single, white female coworker continuously gets brownie points for working late and is considered a valuable resource. You are always at least one hour early each morning. Yet, you are viewed as "not committed" because you leave at 5 p.m. each day.

You know you're "black" in corporate america when...

You are asked why so many newly hired staff of color have unique names. "Is it because they like attention? You need to ask so often if the pronunciation is correct."

You know you're "black" in corporate america when...

A recent wave of thefts has hit your department. The extra security forces have worn the carpet thin leading to your office.

You know you're "black" in corporate america when...

You are asked to give some of your key clients to a coworker with less qualifications and skill level so that she "can come up to speed more quickly." Six months later this same person replaces you.

You know you're "black" in corporate america when...

You ask to check out the shared office laptop for a special project. You are asked by the supply room supervisor why you need it and whether you know how to use it.

You know you're "black" in corporate america when...

You work three or four times as hard before you get recognition.

If any.

You know you're "black" in corporate america when...

You and about six other high profile men and women are relocated to the company's headquarter city and you discover that the group is lovingly called "The Black Breakfast club" when referred to by other peer groups.

You know you're "black" in corporate america when...

You are expected at a company social gathering to be 'Debbie Allen' and teach everyone the latest dance steps. One coworker innocently says, "We could not wait for you to get here. We know *you* know how to dance!"

You know you're "black" in corporate america when...

You hesitate about wearing your new outfit to the office. Today is not the day to answer questions about where you bought it, how much it cost, and if you robbed a bank to pay for it!

You know you're "black" in corporate america when...

You and your executive team are heading to a meeting in your top managers' car. The vehicle has a flat tire. They all look at you, expecting you to change it.

You know you're "black" in corporate america when...

You return from a business trip to Africa. You are asked by a peer who sees you a credible competitor; "Would Africa be a place for you to consider a relocation opportunity?"

You know you're "black" in corporate america when...

You have finished a project well ahead of your fellow peers in a training class, led by a "brother" instructor. You are asked in an implied manner whether you have some kind of "inside edge" because of your [racial] relationship with the instructor?

You know you're "black" in corporate america when...

It is assumed that your role models are athletes like Michael Jordan or Jackie Joyner Kersee, not business executives such as Robert Johnson of BET, Oprah Winfrey of Harpo Productions, Barry Rand of Xerox, Loida Lewis and the late Reginald Lewis of TLC Beatrice Holdings, Kenneth Chenault of American Express, Herman Cain of Godfather's, Earl Graves of Black Enterprise, Maria Dowd of Promotrends, Linda Keene of American Express, Richard Parsons of Time Warner, or Lloyd Ward of Maytag.

...and on and on and on...

You know you're "black" in corporate america when...

You are expected to plan the year end office party, year after year, after year, after year.

You know you're "black" in corporate america when...

You are constantly mistaken for the other "sistah" who has an office on your floor.

There is no resemblance.

You know you're "black" in corporate america when...

Your first name is arbitrarily shortened to one or two syllables (Rich, Kath, Mel, Deb) with out your permission.

And you don't like it!

You know you're "black" in corporate america when...

The newly hired director discovers that your salary is higher than his. From that day forward everything changes drastically; nothing you do is satisfactory, or acceptable.

You become the enemy.

You know you're " black " in corporate america when...

Your white male peer confides in you that the corporation's diversity goals hurt those who are too young to have ever had the opportunity to discriminate ....

...yet.

You know you're "black" in corporate america when...

You see a new male colleague wipe his hands on his pants after he shakes your hand at your welcome reception.

You know you're "black" in corporate america when...

You are the only woman of color executive at a board of directors meeting. The meeting begins and the administrative assistant is not in attendance. The president immediately asks you to take notes until she returns.

You know you're "black" in corporate america when...

Your white coworker does not understand why you are "s-o-o-o sensitive" and will not let "just any photographer" take your official corporate photograph.

You know you're "black" in corporate america when...

You are asked every summer if black people tan.

You know you're "black" in corporate america when...

You realize during a Monday morning coffee break that everyone was invited to a colleague's summer cabin for the weekend, except you.

You know you're "black" in corporate america when...

You go for the first time with coworkers for the monthly "men's night only". They begin "scoping" the girls in the crowd and spot one that they all are crazy about. She walks over and asks *you* to dance. When you return to the group, you are asked with disgust "Are you trying to move in on our p___y base already?"

You know you're "black" in corporate america when...

You are hired into an accelerated management training program, noted for its history of choosing the best and brightest of the company's young managers. After three months, you discover that your colleagues are all matched with informal mentors, and have already had many executive networking opportunities.

Somehow, you missed out.

You know you're "black" in corporate america when...

You spend too much energy and time trying to constantly prove yourself on the job, instead of maximizing your potential and achieving more productivity.

You know you're "black" in corporate america when...

One of your colleagues takes the last cup of coffee, then passes by five others in the conference room to ask you to make a fresh pot.

You know you're "black" in corporate america when...

The first Rodney King police brutality trial jury's *not guilty* verdict was announced, and your colleagues avoided you for the entire week.

You know you're "black" in corporate america when...

Your colleague complains about the 3% raise that he just received, while you were being told that although your performance is excellent, your raise is at zero percent due to the recent department decisions regarding salary range limits.

"Keep up the good work we'll see what we can do next year."

You know you're "black" in corporate america when...

You have an excellent physique. A male colleague squeezes your arm and says. "You're in good shape, you must work out every day!" Later you hear that he tells another coworker," I wonder if his mind is as strong as his body appears to be. We'll find out soon."

You know you're "black" in corporate america when...

Your presentation to the board was finally accepted after many attempts by others in your department. Back in your office, you are so ecstatic that you raise your hands and say "Praise the Lord!" Your manager says "Why? You did the work!"

You know you're "black" in corporate america when...

101 JUST WON'T DO!
READ ON, THERE'S MORE ....

The O.J. Simpson murder trial just came to an end, and you're the only one in the office asked if you truly thought that O.J. didn't do it!

You know you're "black" in corporate america when...

You are promoted from a nonmanagement to a supervisory position, and your manager says, "I want you to know that we did not promote you simply because you are black!"

You know you're "black" in corporate america when...

You receive a call from an out of town family member informing you that your mother just had a stroke and is in a coma. You share the news with your manager and ask for a few days off. You are granted the time off and in the same breath your manager asks, "How do you plan to make up for the time?"

You know you're "black" in corporate america when...

Your peers have 'wonderful' weekends and you have 'Just a couple of days off.'

You know you're "black" in corporate america when...

In your exit interview, you respond with the only 'truths' you can share, "This experience has been very valuable. It is one that I will never forget. I've learned a lot. Thank you for the opportunity."

You know you're "black" in corporate america when...

You walk into a room, and everyone stops talking.

You know you're "black" in corporate america when...

After several of your coworkers have returned from a weekend in the sun, they run to you on Monday morning and ask you to hold out your arm. They extend their arms to touch yours and say, "Hey, I'm darker than you!"

You know you're "black" in corporate america when...

Walking through the hall with a coworker, you exchange greetings with two other blacks you pass along the way. Your coworker says in amazement, "My, you know so many people!"

You know you're "black" in corporate america when...

You are told that your attitude is affecting others in the office. You are asked to "..... lighten up and not be so serious about the work. Smile and laugh more often, to make others more comfortable with you."

You know you're "black " in corporate america when...

You've worked for the company for over two years. During a meeting with your boss you express a desire to pursue a higher level position you've been preparing for all along. Your boss says, "Do you think you are ready for such responsibilities?"

You know you're "black" in corporate america when...

Your company experiences a major reorganization. Your mentor/ sponsor is assigned an international assignment in London and she recruits all of your colleagues, except you. You are left with no immediate options.

You know you're "black" in corporate america when...

You and two colleagues are aboard a flight. The airplane is experiencing problems and returns to the airport. Upon landing you call your family first. Your colleagues' first calls are to the boss.

You know you're "black" in corporate america when...

You move to your new suite on the executive floor and all of the other officers go berserk. From day one, they all scheme to get you a "much nicer office" on another floor.

You know you're "black" in corporate america when...

A VP, known for diversity and bringing high numbers of people of color into the division is fired. Within two weeks, the new black employees are assigned to the company's lowest performing product division.

You know you're "black" in corporate america when...

You realize that at times you must 'dumb down' appearing to be dependent and unaware, so that your manager and peers feel that they are helping you and playing a key role in your development and success.

You know you're "black" in corporate america when...

You assumed that all that was required of you was to work hard and get the job done.

You know you're "black" in corporate america when...

Your boss won't support you for the next promotion opportunity because according to a coworker, you are not considered a "team player". Apparently, the word is out that "all she does is work at her desk, she never spends time with us." In a three day team building session later, you learn that you need to "Go to lunch and coffee with your peers to make them feel like you want to be around them," and then you'll get your promotion.

Surprise—
You thought hard work and dedication made the difference!

You know you're "black" in corporate america when...

You file an EEO complaint. No one talks to you. No new projects are assigned to you. You are constantly criticized for everything.

You know you're "black" in corporate america when...

You have to justify your decision over and over again when you promote another African American male to an officer position.

You know you're "black" in corporate america when...

You are in a private meeting with your boss. The secretary walks in and begins a conversation. Your boss reminds the secretary that she is in a meeting. He says, "Oh, I knew that, but I also saw who you were with and didn't think that he would mind. Sorry."

You know you're "black" in corporate america when...

You have to perform at 250 percent just to stay even.

You know you're "black" in corporate america when...

You have to document everything. You've learned the hard way.

You know you're "black" in corporate america when...

You know racism is a painful reality for you and just the ugly "R word" for others who don't want to discuss it.

You know you're "black" in corporate america when...

A promotion for them equals a pay raise and career advancement. For you it's a pay raise and a new set of business cards.

You know you're "black" in corporate america when...

You have to determine if your boss, peer or employee's racist action is motivated by mistake, ignorance or intent. You ask yourself, "Do I correct them or educate them?" or "Maybe I should just bust 'em right now!"

You know you're "black" in corporate america when...

Your white colleagues are rewarded and considered tough when they rant, rave, slam doors and throw papers, but such actions by you are labeled "out of control and unprofessional".

You know you're "black" in corporate america when...

You are charged with preparing an important report and the person who is responsible for "crunching the numbers" takes a couple days off intentionally to sabotage your efforts.

You know you're "black" in corporate america when...

You return from vacation the day before your big presentation to the board of directors only to find your desk ransacked and your sales forecast and results missing. Your peer peeks in and says, "I bet you were looking for this, weren't you? The cleaning person found it in the break room trash can and suspected it was tossed out by mistake."

You know you're "black" in corporate america when...

You must always throw your coffee away after it has been sitting on your desk unattended. You never know when one of your "friends" may want to add a little something to it.

You know you're "black" in corporate america when...

You are finally promoted, but before it is effective your boss pulls the offer. One of his college buddies has relocated and needs a job.

You know you're "black" in corporate america when...

You have just been hired to take over a new department. Your entire staff has been selected for you, including your personal secretary "Ms Suzy Seductive" who obviously wears no underwear. She intentionally brushes against you at least three times a day.

You know if you take the bait, you are history and she gets a bonus!

You know you're "black" in corporate america when...

After a heated discussion about the value of diversity, one of your fellow board members pats you on the back and says, "With your personality, I am sure you were able to schmooze your way through corporate America. You were able to get great assignments and move right up the ladder with no problems! Right?"

Yeah right!

You know you're "black" in corporate america when...

You give a deposition during the investigation of another employee, but all the questions are about your personal life.

The target of the investigation is really you.

Lessons Learned...

Words of Wisdom for your success

The following words of wisdom are a few lessons learned, passed on to you from those whose experiences are captured in this book. Hopefully, this will help you shorten your learning curve as you may experience being ....''black'' in corporate america.

- Strengthen your relationship with GOD!

- Never say no to doing things outside of your job, don't restrict yourself to your job description.

- Understand the politics and the political game, and that you don't have to play it.

- Know and understand the ramifications if you choose or choose not to play the political game.

- Don't lose sight of who you are!

Lessons Learned...

Words of Wisdom for your success

- Network, Network and Network!!!!!!!!

- Observe the unwritten rules,
  the things that people don't tell you.

- Know who to go to lunch or coffee with.

- Manage your communications upwards.

- Know that you have options.

- Plan, do, check and act.

- Think beyond your self, see yourself as a mentor,
  give back what you've learned.

- Know that everything is based on relationships.

- Don't let anger get the best of you. Develop
  coping skills.

Lessons Learned...

Words of Wisdom for your success

- Figure out a way to have fun.

- Don't make the bumps a serious mountain.

- Don't take the disappointments seriously. Reflect for a moment and learn from them.

- Be your own person.

- Say often, "This too shall pass."

- Focus on the learnings from each situation.

- Know that the situation is only for the moment at hand and not forever.

- Understand your anger and where it comes from.

- Understand your tolerance level. Get to stepping if that level is reached often.

Lessons Learned...

Words of Wisdom for your success

- Document, document, document! Document meetings, outcomes and feedback. Keep your own records.

- Seek help and support. It's there, take advantage of it.

- Always have a plan "B".

- Understand that all expectations can not be met, minimize your disappointments....

- Move out of your comfort zone.

- Know who you can trust, and who not to trust.

- Seek to find the commonalities, lower the fence, remove barriers, find the connection.

- Learn from the mistakes of others, don't repeat them.

- Stay connected to community.

Lessons Learned...

Words of Wisdom for your success

- Balance the perks, pressure, performance and prestige.

- Don't be afraid to mentor, support, be honest with those new to the game.

- Maintain courage and integrity. Do the right thing always.

- Read the "handwriting on the wall" and take heed.

- One's piece of mind is more valuable than a big title!

- Climb the hurdles for your own satisfaction.

- Once you've reached that goal,
  there's yet another hurdle to climb.

- Don't allow others' perceptions of you
  limit your possibilities.

- Maintain your sense of enthusiasm.

Lessons Learned...

Words of Wisdom for your success

- Remain confident and proactive.

- Respect yourself and those around you.

- Don't get upset or get set up.

- Timing is everything.

- Play by the rules.

- Believe that you are qualified and are worthy.

- If necessary vent anger one on one,
  it's your word against theirs.

- Control your temper and ego.

- Investigate the scope of the job before accepting it.

Lessons Learned...

Words of Wisdom for your success

- Don't give up too soon!

- Maintain your self worth.

- Know that you are enough.

- Can't move up, then consider shipping out.

- Build a relationship with an executive recruiter.

- Don't get angry, get even by forgiving!

- Strengthen your relationship with GOD!

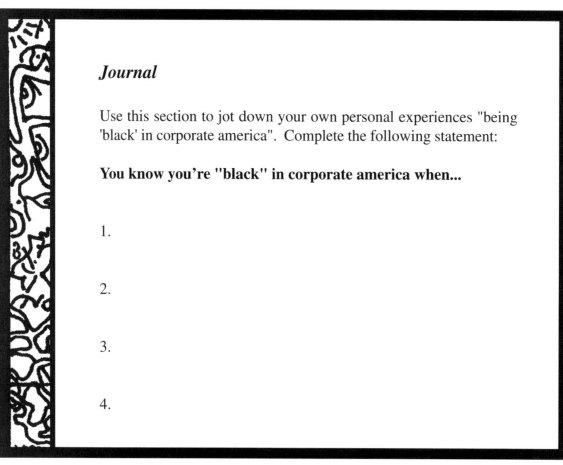

Journal

Use this section to jot down your own personal experiences "being 'black' in corporate america". Complete the following statement:

You know you're "black" in corporate america when...

1.

2.

3.

4.

*To share journal entries for possible inclusion in the next edition of **101 Ways** ... write:*
Watts-Five Productions 1400-F HWY 101 North Suite 117   Plymouth, Minnesota 55447

Journal

5.

6.

7.

8.

9.

10.

Authors Note:

The word "black" found in the title and throughout this book is artfully applied to define the manner in which African Americans and people of color are treated in corporate America. It is my experience that words can be very powerful and can create conditions. The word " black" is no exception. Found in the word black is the word "lack", meaning deficient, inadequate or insufficient. In our society the cultural norm dictates that to be "black" is to "lack". In corporate America, that same perception exists. African Americans and people of color are treated as though there is something lacking. The general use/application of the word "black" in this book is inclusive. It refers to any situation where anyone of any color can be "black" in corporate America, when they are treated differently. The use of the term in *"101 ways..."* and the statement, *" You know you're black in corporate america when..."* highlights the downsides of that perception. By no means do I support the negative notion of lack or inadequacy in regard to people of color, African Americans or other persons of African origin. Nothing is further from the truth!

I do believe that, what is lacking is the insertion of the true gifts of our blackness in corporate America. At times we are guilty of leaving our blackness at the corporation's doorstep, while often adhering to a sense of lacking. Although, there are many times when it is difficult to make sense of the experiences we have in life or in corporate America, we cannot own, believe, or accept that this is due to something that is lacking within us.. Let's not buy into the notion that we are unworthy, or incomplete, or lacking what it takes to be successful in the corporate arena. Some of us try too hard to change who we are because we think we are not educated enough, not good enough, and even........... not white enough!

As we move into the next millennium we need to be careful not to accept the society's subtle definition of the word. Let's aggressively and proudly insert/ affirm the true meaning of "Black" in all that we do. We too are the sons and daughters of the Creator. GOD has blessed us with the gift of our blackness to enhance the universe. Being Black means having the gift of strength, spirit and family. GOD has made us all worthy and complete.

Remember the words of author Iyanla Vanzant, in <u>Acts of Faith</u>. "We cannot change the color of our skin. We can change how we feel about it. We cannot change our pain-filled past. We can change how it affects us. We cannot change how others may feel about who we are. We can change how we feel about what they feel. The past has already been written, but we have the power to write the future."

In my personal life I use and prefer to be known as African American in honor of the blood of my African ancestry running through my veins. I also acknowledge that the use of the word black in our society also refers to the descendants of Africans, living in North America, the Caribbean, Latin America, and Africa.

The names, professions and all other identifying information relating to the persons who so generously shared their stories with me, will remain confidential. Some of the situations have been altered to protect the privacy of those individuals. Any similarity between these stories/situations and any living person is purely coincidental.

To order additional copies of
101 ways to know you're "black" in corporate america
send check or money order for $15.95
(includes shipping, handling & tax) to:

Watts-Five Productions
1400-F HWY 101 North Suite 117
Plymouth, Minnesota 55447

or

Call *the "black" in corporate america hotline: 612-891-6545*

You may also contact the author through the *"black" in corporate america hotline* to arrange public appearances and book signings.

About the Author

Deborah A. Watts, a native of Omaha Nebraska and marketing and sales professional, spent over 20 years in corporate America in the data and telecommunication industry. Currently, she is the founder and president of Watts-Five Productions, a marketing consulting company. She parlays her experience and expertise by assisting entrepreneurs, small businesses, publishers, and nonprofit organizations in building and executing their marketing plans and strategies. Her academic and professional background include organizational development and communications, psychology and numerous advanced executive development programs. The author is dedicated to her community and devotes her time to many professional and civic affiliations including, The Alliance of Black Telecommunication Professionals, St. Paul Urban League, Rotary International, International Leadership Institute, and the National Black MBA Association. Ms. Watts currently resides in Plymouth, Minnesota. Deborah is a devoted wife, mother of three beautiful daughters and proud grandmother of one grandson. Her passion for life and search for creative ways to build bridges of understanding are driven and inspired by the untimely death of family member Emmett Till, her former corporate career and travels to South Africa. She is living testimony of how good GOD is. Deborah's energy, drive and determination have inspired many to live their lives to the fullest. She continuously challenges herself and others to aggressively pursue their purpose and dreams.